Introducing Continents

Africa

Chris Oxlade

Heinemann
LIBRARY

Chicago, Illinois

© 2014 Heinemann Library
an imprint of Capstone Global Library, LLC
Chicago, Illinois

To contact Capstone Global Library please phone 800-747-4992, or visit our web site, www.capstonepub.com

Edited by Dan Nunn, Rebecca Rissman, Sian Smith, and Helen Cox Cannons
Designed by Philippa Jenkins
Original illustrations © Capstone Global Library Ltd 2014
Picture research by Liz Alexander and Tristan Leverett
Production by Vicki Fitzgerald
Originated by Capstone Global Library Ltd
Printed and bound in China by Leo Paper Products Ltd

17 16 15 14 13
10 9 8 7 6 5 4 3 2 1

Library of Congress Cataloging-in-Publication Data
Oxlade, Chris.
    Introducing Africa / Chris Oxlade.
        p. cm.—(Introducing continents)
    Includes bibliographical references and index.
    ISBN 978-1-4329-8038-2 (hb)—ISBN 978-1-4329-8046-7 (pb) 1. Africa—Juvenile literature. I. Title. II. Series: Introducing continents.

DT3.O97 2013
916—dc23   2012049450

Acknowledgments
The author and publisher are grateful to the following for permission to reproduce copyright material: Alamy pp. 19 (© imagebroker); Corbis pp. 18 (© Andrew Aitchison/In Pictures), 26 (© George Steinmetz); Getty Images pp. 11 (Nigel Pavitt/AWL Images), 16 (Mint Images - Frans Lanting), 27 (Issouf Sanogo/AFP); naturepl.com p. 15 (© Nick Garbutt); Shutterstock pp. 6 (© N Mrtgh), 7 (© Przemyslaw Skibinski), 8 (© ricardomiguel.pt), 9 (© Graeme Shannon), 10 (© bumihills), 12 (© POZZO DI BORGO Thomas), 13 (© Vadim Petrakov), 14 (© Eric Isselee), 17 (© Rechitan Sorin), 21 (© Wessel du Plooy), 23 (© Frontpage), 24 (© Steve Heap), 25 (© urosr); SuperStock p.20 (Tips Images).

Cover photographs of Mt Kilimanjaro at sunrise, Massai Warriors in Tanzania, and shaded relief map of Africa all reproduced with permission of Shutterstock (© javarman, © Hector Conesa, © AridOcean).

Every effort has been made to contact copyright holders of any material reproduced in this book. Any omissions will be rectified in subsequent printings if notice is given to the publisher.

Disclaimer
All the Internet addresses (URLs) given in this book were valid at the time of going to press. However, due to the dynamic nature of the Internet, some addresses may have changed, or sites may have changed or ceased to exist since publication. While the author and publisher regret any inconvenience this may cause readers, no responsibility for any such changes can be accepted by either the author or the publisher.

Contents

Some words are shown in bold, **like this**. You can find out what they mean by looking in the glossary.

About Africa

Africa is one of the world's seven **continents**. A continent is a huge area of land. Africa is the second largest continent. Half of Africa is north of the **equator**, and half is south of the equator.

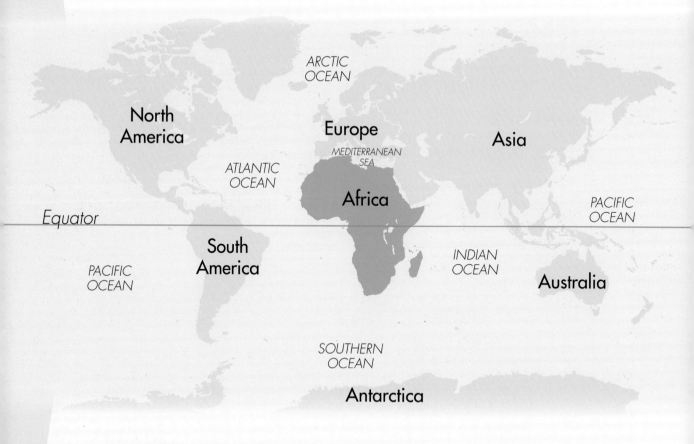

ARCTIC
OCEAN

North
America

Europe

Asia

ATLANTIC
OCEAN

MEDITERRANEAN
SEA

Africa

PACIFIC
OCEAN

Equator

PACIFIC
OCEAN

South
America

INDIAN
OCEAN

Australia

SOUTHERN
OCEAN

Antarctica

Africa is almost surrounded by water. To the west is the Atlantic Ocean. To the east is the Indian Ocean. The Mediterranean Sea is to the north. The huge island of Madagascar is also part of Africa.

Africa Fact File	
Area	About 11,724,000 square miles (30,365,000 square kilometers)
Population	More than 1 billion
Number of countries	56
Highest mountain	Kilimanjaro at 19,341 feet (5,895 meters)
Longest river	Nile River at 4,132 miles (6,650 kilometers)

Famous Places

You might have heard of some of the famous places in Africa. Some of these places are ancient. The pyramids are in Egypt, near the city of Cairo. Ancient Egyptians built them about 4,500 years ago.

This photograph shows the Sphinx and the Great Pyramid.

The local name of the Victoria Falls is Mosi-oa-Tunya, which means "smoke that thunders."

The Victoria Falls are on the Zambezi River, between the countries of Zambia and Zimbabwe. They are 5,604 feet (1,708 meters) wide, and 324 feet (99 meters) high.

Geography

In the north and south of Africa are vast **deserts**, with huge sand dunes. The Sahara Desert covers almost all of North Africa. The Namib Desert and the Kalahari Desert are in the south.

The Sahara Desert is the largest hot desert in the world.

Atlas Mountains

Sahara Desert

Mount Kenya

Ruwenzori Range

Mount Kilimanjaro

Namib Desert

Kalahari Desert

Drakensberg Mountains

0	600 miles
0	965 km

8

Kilimanjaro is a **volcano**, but it does not erupt anymore.

There are vast grassy plains in Africa, called grasslands. Along the **equator** there are rain forests. Kilimanjaro and Mount Kenya are the two highest mountains in Africa. They are in East Africa.

The Nile is the longest river in the world. It starts in the middle of Africa and flows all the way to the Mediterranean Sea. Other great rivers in Africa are the Congo, Niger, and Zambezi.

The Nile River flows through the desert in Egypt.

MEDITERRANEAN SEA

Nile River

Senegal River

Niger River

Congo River

Lake Victoria

ATLANTIC OCEAN

INDIAN OCEAN

Zambezi River

Limpopo River

| 0 | 600 miles |
| 0 | 965 km |

Orange River

These fishermen are preparing their boats on the shores of Lake Victoria.

Lake Victoria is the largest lake in Africa. It is also the second largest lake in the world. It measures 209 miles (337 kilometers) from north to south and 149 miles (240 kilometers) from west to east. More than 200 different types of fish live in the lake.

Weather

In much of Africa, the weather is warm or hot most of the time. Along the **equator**, the weather is **tropical**. It is hot and wet all year round. It rains almost every day in the rain forests.

Trees and other plants grow well in the warm, wet tropical weather.

Heavy rain showers move across the African plains during the rainy season.

In the grasslands, there is a dry season, when it never rains, and a rainy season, when it rains almost every day. In the **deserts**, it is dry year-round. It is very hot in the daytime but cold at night.

Animals

An amazing variety of animals live in Africa. Elephants, giraffes, rhinoceroses, and lions live on the grasslands. There are also big herds of zebras, wildebeests, and antelopes. Gorillas live in the rain forests.

Herds of wildebeests and elephants live on the African plains.

These ring-tailed lemurs live in a nature reserve in Madagascar.

Madagascar is a large island on the east coast of Africa. Most of the animals that live there don't live anywhere else on Earth. The most famous are the lemurs.

Plants

Many unusual plants grow in Africa. Plants grow very well in the wet, warm rain forests. There are huge trees, such as mahogany trees and ebony trees. There are also amazing plants, such as orchids and African violets.

These beautiful orchids are growing in the rain forest in Madagascar.

Palm trees grow in the desert where water comes up from underground.

Baobab trees with thick trunks and thorny acacia trees stand in the grasslands. Palm trees grow at **oases** in **deserts**. Papyrus grows along the banks of the Nile River. The ancient Egyptians used papyrus to write on like paper.

People

There are hundreds of different groups of people living in different parts of Africa. Big groups include Arabs and Berbers in North Africa. Some small groups of people, such as the Mbuti, live in the rain forests.

Mbuti pygmies live in the Democratic Republic of Congo. They hunt animals and gather plants.

Many different languages are spoken in Morocco, including Arabic, Berber and French.

More than 1,500 different languages are spoken in Africa. People have spoken these African languages for thousands of years. In many African countries, people also speak English, Portuguese, French, or Arabic.

African Culture

Many African people still do their traditional dances on special occasions. They dress in traditional costumes and some wear body paint. Masai men in East Africa perform a special jumping dance.

These Chuka people from Kenya play traditional music on drums.

Most towns and villages in Africa have a dirt soccer field.

Soccer is the most popular sport in Africa. Every two years the national soccer teams of African countries play in the Africa Cup of Nations. Cricket is played in South Africa, Zimbabwe, and Kenya.

Countries

There are 56 countries in Africa. Algeria, in North Africa, is the largest. The Seychelles in the Indian Ocean is the smallest. It is made up of many islands.

This map shows the countries of Africa.

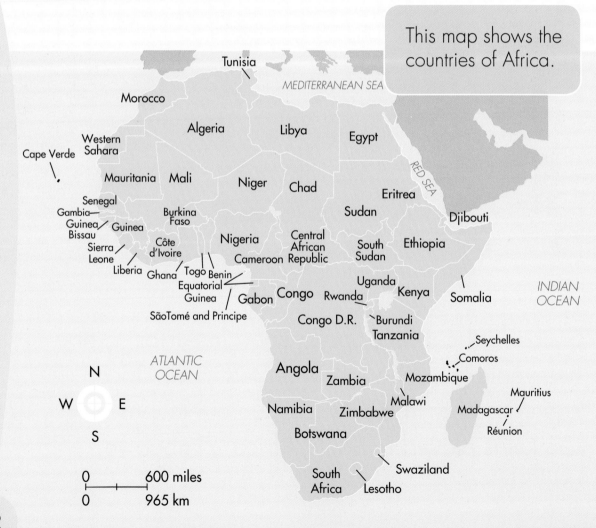

Tunisia

MEDITERRANEAN SEA

Morocco

Algeria Libya Egypt

Western Sahara

Cape Verde

RED SEA

Mauritania Mali Niger Chad

Eritrea

Senegal Sudan Djibouti

Gambia Burkina Faso
Guinea Guinea
Bissau

Sierra Leone Nigeria Central African Republic South Sudan Ethiopia

Côte d'Ivoire

Liberia Ghana Togo Benin
Cameroon

Uganda Kenya

INDIAN OCEAN

Equatorial Guinea Congo Rwanda Somalia

SãoTomé and Principe Gabon

Congo D.R. Burundi Tanzania

Seychelles

Comoros

ATLANTIC OCEAN

Angola Mozambique Mauritius

N

W E

Zambia

S

Namibia Zimbabwe Malawi Madagascar Réunion

Botswana

0 ——— 600 miles
0 ——— 965 km

South Africa Lesotho Swaziland

22

Juba is the capital of South Sudan, which is Africa's newest country.

Countries from Europe once ruled most of Africa. That is why people in some African countries speak English or French. A new African country was made in 2011, when South Sudan split away from the rest of Sudan.

Cities and Countryside

Four in every ten Africans live in a city. Cairo, the capital city of Egypt, is the African city with the greatest number of people. Eleven million people live there. Many people live in **slums**, without electricity or running water.

This is a view over the rooftops of Cairo, the capital of Egypt.

In many African villages, people get water from their village well.

In the countryside, people live in small villages. Many make a living from farming or by looking after herds of animals. Some also find food by hunting animals and gathering plants.

Natural Resources and Products

Africa has many **natural resources**. Oil is found under the ground in North Africa and West Africa. Nigeria produces the most oil of any country in Africa. Diamonds and gold are mined from the ground in South Africa.

These are oil wells on the banks of the Niger River in Nigeria.

A farmer in the Ivory Coast cuts down pods full of cocoa beans.

Farmers grow crops for themselves, to sell at market, or to send to other countries. Bananas, yams, coffee, tea, and peanuts are popular crops to grow. Most of the world's cocoa beans come from West Africa. They are turned into chocolate.

Fun Facts

- The Great Rift Valley is a huge valley in East Africa. It is 4,000 miles (6,400 kilometers) long and up to 60 miles (100 kilometers) wide.

- The Suez Canal carries huge ships 101 miles (163 kilometers) across the **desert** between the Red Sea and the Mediterranean Sea.

- A large amount of the world's gold comes from mines in South Africa.

- The cheetah lives on the grasslands of Africa. It can reach a speed of 70 miles (113 kilometers) per hour when it is chasing **prey**.

Quiz

1. Which African river is the longest river in the world?

2. Which city are the pyramids at Giza close to?

3. On which island do lemurs live?

4. What grows in Africa that chocolate comes from?

4. The cocoa bean

3. Madagascar

2. Cairo, in Egypt

1. The Nile

Glossary

continent one of seven huge areas of land on Earth

desert area of land that gets very little rain

equator imaginary line running around the middle of Earth

natural resources natural materials that we use, such as wood, coal, oil, and rock

oases places in a desert where plants can grow because there is water just under the ground

prey animal that is hunted and eaten by another animal

slums overcrowded area of a city where poor people live

tropical place near the equator where the weather is hot and rainy all year

volcano mountain with a hole in the top that ash or hot melted rock comes out of

Find Out More

Books

Royston, Angela and Michael Scott. *Africa's Most Amazing Plants*. Chicago: Raintree, 2008.

Schaefer, A.R. *Spotlight on Africa*. Mankato, Minn.: Capstone, 2011.

Underwood, Deborah. *Exploring Africa*. Chicago: Heinemann, 2007.

Web sites

FactHound offers a safe, fun way to find Internet sites related to this book. All of the sites on FactHound have been researched by our staff.

Here's all you do:
Visit www.facthound.com
Type in this code: 9781432980382

Index